BLUFF YOUR WAY
ON
THE INTERNET

ROBERT AINSLEY

G000150261

ЯR
RAVETTE PUBLISHING

Published by Ravette Publishing Limited
P.O. Box 296
Horsham
West Sussex RH13 8FH

Telephone: (01403) 711443
Fax: (01403) 711554

First printed 1996
Reprinted 1996
Revised 1997
Reprinted 1997

Series Editor – Anne Tauté

Cover design – Jim Wire, Quantum
Printing & binding – Cox & Wyman Ltd.
Production – Oval Projects Ltd.

The Bluffer's Guides™ series is based
on an original idea by Peter Wolfe.

The Bluffer's Guides™, Bluffer's™
and Bluff Your Way™ are Trademarks.

An Oval Project
for Ravette Publishing.

CONTENTS

INTRODUCTION

The Internet, the Information Superhighway, Cyberspace, the World Wide Web – all describe the same simple idea: computers linked by telephone lines. But, like any good con artist, the Internet uses several names, each designed to deceive in different ways.

a) **The Internet**. It suggests a highly-organised, supportive community, socialising over the network of millions of computers. Once, computer users were sad, isolated people, spending solitary lives at keyboards. Now, the Internet has put everyone's computers in contact with each other – so we can all be sad, isolated people spending solitary lives at keyboards.

b) **Information Superhighway**. It sounds as if all sorts of exciting facts can be speedily and freely picked up: text, sound, graphics, reference material, personal and business mail. But it's more like a permanent roadworks: slow, frustrating, chaotic and full of people shaking their fists at each other.

c) **Cyberspace**. It implies a dream world, where everything is worked out on computers to be the ideal solution. Global peace and understanding are promoted, virtual reality makes real life better, and everyone has perfect teeth.

In fact, like real space, it consists largely of a vacuum, with occasional patches of explosive matter. By bringing together misfits, perverts and extremists it has spread more hate than the average civil war. Real reality has only one thing in common with virtual reality: as you move around them, both are full of unpleasant jerks. And few Internet users could model for toothpaste ads – to judge by the bite patterns they leave on their keyboards as they wait in frustration for a twenty-minute page to load.

d) **World Wide Web**. It promotes the image of a wonderfully simple yet elegant structure of communication, which looks beautiful and magical in the right light. In fact it's the section of the Internet which displays pictures, text, sound and even interactive programs in a magazine-page-like way.

You would think from its name that such a web would be able to catch anything of interest. Not a bit of it. It's sticky, messy, full of indigestible little bits, and the owner probably left for another site two years ago.

However, the Internet has one highly important quality. People believe it must be interesting.

Unlike normal computing – which is important and useful – the Internet is trivial and virtually useless, but a fascinating way to waste all that spare time you have now that your job has been taken by a computer.

Thus its greatest appeal is to people who are themselves fascinating, but trivial and useless – that is, journalists, who therefore write copiously about the Internet, ensuring its continued reputation. (Few of those who write about the Internet have ever actually used it, of course. This is because few of those who use the Internet can write, a fact demonstrated by what you see in newsgroups.)

There is one more vital quality of the Internet.

Everything about it is true.

Every story, every rumour, every article made up by hurried hacks – it's all true. And if it isn't now, then it will be by the year 2006. You need not restrict yourself to facts or reality – nobody contributing to newsgroups does. You can make up absolutely anything: how you browsed a newsgroup for owners of pet boa constrictors, read the Pentagon computer's plans for World War III, got an e-mail from the Pope, or watched a real-time video of a famous Hollywood star doing suggestive things with a cauliflower.

It will be not only plausible, but impressive. And no-one, not even an expert, will be able to disprove you. Not even those with a specialist knowledge of snakes or garden vegetables.

The Internet has no inventor or pioneer, no heroes, no household names, and no great popularisers. So, whoever the other person mentions enthusiastically can be dismissed as "overrated and insignificant", which will always be right.

This makes the Internet the ideal subject to bluff about. You will sound clever, informed, and right up to date. And by not actually using it, you will also save yourself unimaginable amounts of money, time and effort.

WHAT THE INTERNET OFFERS

There are various kinds of service available via the Internet. Here are five, which is rather more than you will ever need to know about (some people only ever use e-mail, others not even that), together with rather more information than you need to know about each.

There are other types of Internet service (drop in terms such as 'Telnet' or 'IRC' if you need to) but should anyone raise them they can be discarded either as "yesterday's thing" or "an idea whose time has not yet come", depending on how you feel.

E-mail

Electronic mail, or **e-mail**, is the one part of the Internet that almost everyone agrees is actually useful, particularly large companies, who can slim down their workforces by dispensing with middle managers. Not only has their reporting function been replaced by e-mail, but their dismissal notices can be e-mailed direct to their computers, neatly saving managers the time and embarrassment of meeting face-to-face.

For many users, e-mail is the Internet. Any computer on the Internet can send a message to any other computer on the Internet. All you have to do is run your e-mail program, type your message, give the address to send it to, and click on a button. It will pop up on the recipient's screen moments later – where it will then sit unanswered for three weeks while they sift through their huge backlog of e-mails built up since the middle managers were dismissed.

Journalists and writers love it, because it means they can send their copy direct to the copy editor's computer – and thus delay sending it until literally the very last minute. Copy editors hate it for the same reason.

Of course the text comes in already typed – which is another reason copy editors hate it, because that means the mistakes and misspellings come in already typed too. But they tolerate it because, merely by clicking on the 'reply' button when the message arrives and typing a zero, they can immediately send the notification of the journalist's fee.

E-mail Style

Because e-mail makes people write to each other rather than phone, you can assert that the art of writing – which was being undermined by the telephone – is no longer dying. It has been killed off completely.

The reason lies in the usually sketchy typing skills of most computer users. To test these skills as little as possible, e-mails are generally brief. Often they consist merely of the previously received message sent back with a 'Yes' or 'OK, 10 tomorrow', or 'bollocks', or similar tag appended.

Many verbless sentences too.

Short paragraphs.

Lots.

Strange word order often too there is also.

Sometimes e-mails are typed entirely in upper case with the 'shift' key down, WHICH YOU SHOULD SAY IS THE EQUIVALENT OF SHOUTING.

Abbreviations

Perhaps the most confusing of habits generated by e-mailers is overuse of the TLA. Wait for the other person to say "Ah yes, the three-letter acronym", and tell them they mean 'abbreviation' rather than 'acronym' (RAM, 'random access memory', is an acronym because it is pronounced as a single word; IBM is an abbreviation because each letter is pronounced separately). And then point out that e-mailers have extended the three letters idea to absurd lengths.

For example, a particularly enthusiastic electronic correspondent might write to you: 'BTW, ISTR you are IMHO the best person to ask. IWBNI we could have lunch. TIA, BCNU. PS: Let's meet ASAP.' And if not, there is nothing to stop you claiming that someone has.

This translates as 'By the way, I seem to recall you are in my humble opinion the best person to ask. It would be nice if we could have lunch. Thanks in advance, be seeing you. Post scriptum: Let's meet and sink a pint.' (The last one is fake, of course, but tell it with a straight enough face and you might get away with it.)

You must deride TLAs, FLAs, SLAs and all the other number of letter acronyms (or abbreviations). They show a mind, you say, which is incapable of writing, able only to shuffle together blocks of other people's ideas.

Cite such bizarre (and genuine) examples as ROFL ('rolls on floor laughing' – it's especially hard to see why this should be in use, given the standard of humour on the Internet); NALOPKT ('not a lot of people know that' – or indeed would guess what it stands for); TNSTAAFL ('there's no such thing as a free lunch' – or a free letter-writing kit, more's the pity) and the unpleasant rejoinder FOAD (a sequence of two activities which sum up the existence of a mayfly).

Never use any of the above in your own e-mails. If you write one accidentally, expand it to the full form ASAP.

E-mail Addresses

To send a piece of e-mail, you have to know the recipient's **e-mail address**. This is a simple line consisting of a name to identify the recipient, an @ symbol, and a sequence of letters and **dots** specifying which computer in the world serves as a letter box.

So, for example, John Smith at Acme Computers might have a simple e-mail address like jsmith@acme.com. He might, but he probably wouldn't. It would more likely be something like:

John.Simon.Michael.Smith@compuserve.com, or
jsm_wp.ptc@software-dev.acmecomp.zipnet.co.uk.

("E-mail, simple?", you can say. "Try dictating *that* over the phone…")

The last letters of an e-mail address denote the country: '.uk' for the UK is obvious, but you can impress people enormously by knowing the less obvious ones such as '.jp' for Japan, '.no' for Norway, '.ve' for Venezuela, '.aq' for Antarctica, and so on. Or indeed just making them up, especially from some obscure third-world republic recently in the news. Slipping in such codes does, however, suggest that you receive e-mail correspondence from all over the world.

The United States, being the place which can squarely be blamed for inventing the Internet, doesn't put '.us', or indeed any designation at all, at the end of its addresses. There is a parallel with postage stamps: uniquely, Great Britain doesn't put its name on its stamps, because to the 19th century Englishman, there was only one country in the world. Modern America feels the same, though with more justification, thanks to the unifying power of the Internet.

There are other letter codes in an e-mail address which show the type of destination, such as '.mil' (military), '.org' (organisation), '.gov' (governmental organisation), '.co' (commercial organisation) and so on. Any address ending just in '.com' or '.edu' is respectively a commercial or educational organisation in America. They have to put 'edu' because, in America, there is no guarantee that a 'university' actually *is* an educational institution. Especially as students these days spend most of their time playing around on the Internet instead of attending lectures.

Signatures

Everyone knows that the more intelligent and educated a person, the less legible their handwriting. Actually this isn't true, it just makes people with bad handwriting feel better. Business correspondence is all word-processed, leaving the writer only one way to display their intelligence: with a really indecipherable signature.

E-mails provide no such opportunity. (How will doctors preserve their traditionally illegible prescriptions when they all have to be done on e-mails?)

Many e-mail programs let you create a signature, which will be put automatically at the bottom of any e-mail sent out by you. But it isn't a normal written signature. E-mail can only cope with ASCII – that is, the standard letters and numbers, a handful of punctuation marks, and little else. There are no accents, no effects such as italic or bold, no unusual characters. ('Unusual', that is, from the point of view of the Americans who devised the system, and who seem unaware that not all countries use dollars. For example, the '£' sign, not infrequently used in the UK, cannot be put into e-mails.) In short, e-mail can only cope with about as many characters as a standard typewriter.

So people create their signatures out of huge patterns of ASCII characters. The effect resembles collapsing scaffolding. A large table of _ and / symbols, dozens of characters across and almost as deep, might when viewed from several feet away create the illusion of a name built up from bricks laid at an angle, for example. At that distance you won't be able to read the e-mail, which may be just as well. Other inventive combinations might attempt to pick out the shape of a smiling face, the USS Enterprise, or a pizza, to reflect the interest of the signatory.

But most signatures stick to conventional text, with some hopeful bordering symbols. They might consist of the person's name, their occupation, e-mail address, some stunning piece of personal information, and a quotation which no doubt means a great deal to the signatory, but which looks rather puzzling when given out of context.

The typical sign-off to a letter, then, might look like this:

13

```
=================================
=       Scott J Cheeseburger     =
=     Program Development Dept,   =
=    Millennium Computers Inc,    =
=         Trivia, Illinois.       =
=    scott@progdev.millennium.com =
=                                 =
=  **** Can YOU beat my record of =
=       making a pizza with 58    =
=         toppings?!?!!  ****      =
=                                 =
=      "Feathers hit the ground    =
=     before the weight can leave  =
=             the air              =
=      – 'Fall on Me' by REM       =
=================================
```

How to Criticise It

You can safely disparage e-mail for either or both of the following reasons:

1. People underuse e-mail, so you have just as many memos, phone calls, faxes and letters, but the additional burden of having to learn the e-mail system and monitor your e-mailbox which is rarely used.

2. People overuse e-mail, so that in place of a single phone call taking five minutes, you have a 'conversation' of perhaps a dozen e-mails, which takes ten minutes to deal with and clogs up your computer.

Discussion Point

Alone among computing areas, e-mail is taken up with enthusiasm by women. Make up any reason for this either approving ("intimacy...privacy...group rapport...more socially worthwhile than playing silly computer games") or disapproving ("it's so they can bitch about other people in the office while pretending to work"), whichever will cause most annoyance.

An Urban Myth to Propagate

"A man I know went on holiday, and set his computer to automatically reply to any incoming e-mail with a message saying he was away. His friend at work did the same, but just as he was leaving, he sent a message to the first man saying he'd be away, not knowing he'd just gone away too.

"So the two computers sent the messages to each other, then replies that they'd received them, then replies that they'd received the replies, and so on, every few seconds. So many messages accumulated that within an hour the company's **server** clogged up and crashed. Cost them half a million pounds. It's true. It was a friend of a friend."

Newsgroups

A huge proportion of the world's Internet computer space, sometimes called Usenet, is devoted to newsgroups: electronic noticeboards, each devoted to some specialist interest. You can ask questions, canvas opinions, pass on a snippet of news, or get advice.

Other users of the newsgroup read what you've posted (NB: you don't send or pin up messages, you post them), and within just a few minutes there will be new postings posted for everyone to read in response to yours – saying your question is stupid, your opinion is worthless, and your news inaccurate and outdated.

If you do get any advice, it will be along the lines of telling you to go jump in the lake. Or, more likely, to do something with your computer which for different reasons would make it equally impossible for you to see your screen while sitting down.

Flaming

Faster than a speeding bulletin, newsgroups put people in touch with other people who share common interests – usually interests such as abuse, confrontation, argument, and Anglo-Saxon words which score heavily in Scrabble. **Flaming** – posting offensive remarks to newsgroups – is taken seriously, of course: some people take it so seriously they practise their swearing and insulting techniques for years.

Indeed, so much libel occurs in newsgroup postings that the law may one day be changed to make the poster responsible for it (rather than the organisation running the service, which is supposed to monitor it but clearly could not have the time to do so). In which case, everyone would have to learn the rudiments of libel law, and – after a few test cases showed the potential of widespread libel claims against posters of actionable messages – every newsgroup would suddenly turn very polite, with no more libel suits ever. This would be a great development, partly for the resulting peace and quiet, but mainly because it would force all those libel lawyers to go out and earn a proper living instead.

The way to get the best out of newsgroups is to browse them to see who is posting the sensible, useful, knowledgeable messages. Make a short-list of just those people (though the list will be short already) and then correspond with them personally by e-mail. Obviously you will need to find the appropriate e-mail address, but in all probability you will know it already. It'll be yours.

Using Newsgroups

On screen, a newsgroup looks like a catalogue of titles. You click on one which looks interesting to view the text of that particular posting. Successive postings in reaction to each other can result in a discussion straying somewhat from the original topic. Titles such as 'Re: Lewd acts with vegetables (was "Recommendations please for best CD of Mahler's Fifth")' are common.

There are newsgroups for every subject area of human interest (and many devoted to non-human ones, with pictures of the animals taking part) so you can make up any you like and probably be right. Their names are usually **alt** or **rec** dot something – invent any reason you like to account for these letters – and the subject is often clear. For example, rec. cucumber.growing, alt.fan.madonna, rec.naked.alpine. mountain.biking, alt.llama.husbandry, etc. Any of these however may be among the pornographic newsgroups, to which access is barred from your work computer.

You need never have used a newsgroup to talk at any length about it, of course. If the person you are talking to can hold down any line of argument without having to write down all the swear words they know in capital letters every two minutes, they are not regular newsgroup users – and hence cannot call your bluffs.

How to Criticise Them

You can safely disparage any newsgroup for either, or both, of the following reasons:

1. The subject area is too broad, so there are far too many messages irrelevant to most people's interest clogging it up, making it slow to load. It should be split into smaller groups.

2. The subject area is too specialised, so there are too few messages from the same old people insulting each other in the same way, making it not worth looking at regularly. It should be combined with other groups to make a more interesting larger one.

Discussion Points

Newsgroups provide the ideal refuge for sad, social inadequates who like to send out abuse from the option-ally anonymous safety of their computers. Say this is a valuable service to society ("they can vent their anger on a screen instead of in a real life situation...gives them purpose in life...completely harmless") or an appalling trend ("people becoming unable to sort differ-ences face to face...dehumanising...encourages confron-tationist values...highly dangerous").

An Urban Myth to Propagate

"There was this man in America. Someone mistakenly heard that he'd died, and posted the news to a few of the newsgroups he had been on. Well, the news spread so quickly – you know what newsgroups are like – that within a day, all the credit card companies, banks, his insurance company and employers, had removed his name from their computers, and his wife got condolence cards from all their friends.

"So they just pretended he had died, collected the insurance money, and emigrated with a new identity. It's true. It was a friend of a friend."

World Wide Web

It is said that dictionaries have to be rewritten to take account of new technology. The word 'browser', for example, now refers to a type of computer program, one which can read documents from the Internet and display them on your computer. The particular feature of a browser is that it displays Internet files in a multimedia way, mixing pictures, graphics, words, headlines, neat tables of figures and text, sounds and animations – even forms to fill in which let you buy things with your credit card. Clearly very different from the traditional sense of the word.

However, *Chambers* defines 'browser' as [one who reads] desultorily'. Look up 'desultory' and it says 'jumping from one thing to another; without rational or logical connection; rambling; hasty; loose'. These entries clearly need no revision for the Internet.

The World Wide Web is the part of the Internet which can be displayed by these browsing programs, and is the main reason behind the extraordinary mushrooming of the Internet in the mid-1990s. Mushrooming, that is, in the sense of 'overnight growth sustained by muck'.

This is because Web pages are a status symbol for the company or individual running them. Not just a few pages with tedious text poorly formatted, as you would get on the Internet otherwise; but interactive, snappily-illustrated affairs displaying headlines, graphics, background patterns and colours a-plenty, and containing imaginatively cross-referenced pages, along with tedious text poorly formatted. In other words, Web pages are all too often not so much a triumph of style over content as a walkover.

URLs

Most people could tell you that once you know the URL of a Web page, you can access it from any Internetted computer in the world merely by typing the URL into your browser. However, fewer people know that 'URL' stands not for 'Uniform Resource Location', as commonly thought, but '...Locator".

Or vice versa. It doesn't matter. Just make sure you tell the other person they're wrong, whichever they say it is, and support your argument with some spurious assertion such as "Well, that's what Microsoft's official guidelines call it, and they make over 98% [or other invented but plausible figure] of all the world's browsers...".

Web Sites

Link together more than one Web page and you have a recipe for sore eyes – hence the term Web **site**. The 'shop window' into which you come first and from which all the other sections can be accessed is called the **home page**, and the bigger the Web site, the smaller the URL of the home page. The bigger the Web site, the more likely it is to have been set up by a large company with the resources to pay professional designers and expert programmers (but invariably amateur writers) to put it together.

Hence, you can tell at a glance how much a Web site is worth visiting: divide the figure 100 by the length of the home page's URL and that gives you an interest rating. Percentage rating, that is. When you consider that all URLs have to begin with 'http:/ /www.' (a handicap of eleven letters) then you have an idea how stimulating most Web sites are.

Understanding URLs

URLs contain similar cryptic sequences of letters to e-mail addresses (.kwiknet.co.uk etc.) but are easy to tell apart. An e-mail address always has the @ symbol in the middle and no / marks. A **URL** never has an @ and, apart possibly from the home page, will be full of / marks. Indeed, a URL can sprawl over several lines: the computer where the site resides may store hundreds of thousands of files, and the / marks help it to sort the files into groups.

Typically, the longer the URL, the fewer people would want the information in it; so if you claim to have found something very obscure and specific on the Internet – say, a list of serial numbers for the bogeys of Great Western goods trains running from Evercreech Junction in 1935 – make up a suitably titanic URL such as http://www.steam-trains. co.uk/~ J.Smith/Great_Western/goods/EvcrchJnctn/35/bogeys. html.

(URLs often contain the ~ mark, a.k.a. a 'tilde' or 'that little squiggly thing'. If the other person calls it the second, insist on the first to make them feel silly and amateurish. If they call it the first, insist on the second, to make them feel academic and pedantic.)

Links

Any text <u>which is underlined</u> on a page – a **hot link** – can be clicked on, and will bring up <u>a new page</u> on screen, with <u>further links</u> of its own, either to <u>other pages</u> in the same site, or <u>outside</u> to those of <u>other individuals</u> or <u>organisations</u>. (Such <u>underlining</u> gets visually tedious, as you can see.) The most popular page in the Internet is the one run by a Mr Error 404, whose message for the world is 'The requested page was not found on this server'.

A file which you can download and then play on your own machine to produce sound is called a **soundbyte**. Or soundbite, or sound byte or sound-bite: whichever version the other person uses, say it should be another, justifying your choice with something like "It's from the Greek/Latin/Anglo Saxon, you know", and "The hyphen/space is essential/unnecessary/dangerous because of file naming conventions on UNIX servers".

A stylish, recently-added web page is said to be 'hot'. A page which is particularly hot is 'cool'. A page which is especially good is 'wicked'. And the more a page is littered with graphics and tables, the more it is said to be 'neat'.

Thus you can make any critical judgement you like about a Web site, and it will never be clear from your description whether you are praising it, damning it, damning it with faint praise, praising it with faint damns, or just making the damn thing up entirely.

How to Criticise Them

You can safely disparage any web page for any of the following reasons, three of which will aways be true:

1. There are far too many graphics, which add nothing and take too long to load – a postcard-sized picture can often take up to a minute, the same time as a long chapter of a book.
2. There are not nearly enough graphics. Mere text by itself, no matter how quickly it loads in comparison, is monotonous; the whole reason for the Web is graphic ability.
3. The pages are too long. Anything more than a screenful is hard to read and requires scrolling. Information should be broken down into more, shorter, less weighty pages.
4. The pages are too short. If you have to keep clicking on hot links all the time, it is too easy to lose the thread. Information should be put together into fewer, longer, weightier pages.
5. The sound files are uncompressed. A minute of sound might take three minutes to load. All sound files should be compressed, using simple, readily available programs, to make them much smaller in size and hence far quicker to load.
6. The sound files are compressed. A minute of compressed sound might take only thirty seconds to load, but the reduction in quality because of compression will ruin the effect. All sound files should be uncompressed to make them actually worth listening to.

Discussion Point

Businesses like to show they are at the cutting edge of technology by having their own web sites, and demonstrate the fact by putting the URL of their home page in their magazine and TV ads. Have a strong view on this embracing of the Internet by commerce, either for it ("The classic Internet principles of openness, informality and giving things away for free will start to make their way into big business"), or against it ("The classic big business principles of secrecy, hierarchy and charging for everything will start to make their way into the Internet").

An Urban Myth to Propagate

"Did you see that advertisement on TV last night? The one that gave the company's Web page URL at the end? Well, the 'person' who runs their Web site is listed in the company's brochures, but it's all a fake. It isn't a person at all. It's just a computer that turns all the company's newsletters, sales reports, catalogues and so on into Web pages automatically.

"And you know what? This 'person' keeps being head-hunted by other companies looking for people to run their own Web sites. ICI offered 'him' eighty thousand and a company car. It's true. It was a friend of a friend."

ftp

File transfer protocol, as its name implies, enables any Internet user to get a file from the computer of any other Internet user without observing the usual protocols society would demand – offensive material for example, such as pornographic images, racist tracts, or sound samples from Richard Clayderman's latest CD.

Most **ftp** use, however, is for less controversial subjects. Though the files it sends to your computer could be obtained in other ways, ftp is fast and efficient for very big files, such as graphics, video, sound samples, or indeed computer programs.

Thus, if you wished to obtain an exceedingly long file from someone else's machine – a list of Italian parliaments since 1970, say – you would use ftp. A very short file, on the other hand – the best of Richard Clayderman, perhaps – might be downloaded directly using your Web browser.

How to Criticise It

You can safely disparage any ftp sites for either of the following reasons:

1. They are disappointing because they don't work. Try to download any of the enticing titles such as 'The pictures that were too shocking for Madonna's book!!' or 'Every scorecard from Yorkshire-Lancashire cricket matches since 1882' and you merely get a message from one of Mr Error 404's relatives.

2. They are disappointing because they work. Try to download any of those enticing titles and you find the contents bear scant resemblance to those promised. Or in the case of Richard Clayderman, exactly what was promised. Invent any example you like; it will probably be true.

Discussion Point

Censorship of information is made almost impossible by ftp. Have strong views one way or the other on the effect this will have on society, based on any figures you care to make up one way ("Did you know that 96% of all ftp'ed files are pornographic? Society is sick, etc.") or the other ("Did you know that 96% of all ftp'ed files are cricket scorecards? Society is sick, etc.").

An Urban Myth to Propagate

"This friend of mine waited until his wife was out at her pottery evening class, and downloaded a bunch of pornographic pictures from an ftp site. When he looked through them, he thought there was something strangely familiar about the nude model.

"And guess what? It was his wife! It wasn't pottery classes at all she'd been going to, but a glamour photography club. It's true. It was a friend of a friend."

Gophers

A **gopher** is the part of the Internet which can 'go for' textual information from large public databases such as those run by NASA or the British Library – in other words, a file-finder. The burrowing-animal imagery is appropriate in terms of the scenic and visual interest enjoyed by a creature which spends most of its life in the dark. On screen, gophers present you with drab lists of files which, when clicked on, lead you to other drab lists of files and, eventually, to long and drab text documents.

For you, there is little ground here worth covering, or indeed burrowing under. Gophers are dull and, as you point out, "They do nothing a Web browser doesn't do". They should be dismissed: "Mm. They've got their doctoral theses all linked to a gopher site. Fascinating stuff – if Roman Fireplace Construction in the Upper Danube and its Effect on Urbanisation Trends in Moesia is what turns you on."

How to Criticise Them

You can safely disparage any gopher sites for either of the following reasons:
1. They are dull.
2. They are unbelievably dull.

Discussion Point

Do gophers enhance or diminish the perceived value of the Internet? You can have views either way ("Enhance it, maybe. I don't really care" or "Diminish it, maybe. I don't really care").

An Urban Myth to Propagate

"This researcher in America was using a gopher to find files relating to his doctoral thesis. He found one in a Japanese university, and guess what? The post-doc there had duplicated virtually his entire research, point for point, and was just about to publish it with a contradictory conclusion, disproving this researcher's theory completely, destroying three years' work. Committed suicide, he did...

"Actually it's not true at all. I made it up. He just finished his research and became an accountant."

EQUIPMENT

Getting going on the Internet is neither easy nor cheap. This is excellent news, as you will never get on the Internet; so the harder and more expensive it is, the more time and money you save.

Basic Requirements

Obviously the first thing not to put on your shopping list is a **computer**. Any decent IBM-compatible PC or Apple Macintosh is an ideal omission. A month's salary saved already. If rumbled, tell people you access the Internet at work. As that's how virtually everybody does it, this will be perfectly credible.

Your second enormous saving is not buying Internet **software and manuals**, which will have ghastly names such as 'Kwik and E-Z Internet™ Made Simple® for Duffers in a Box®™©'. The longer the title, the shorter the contents. The more superscripts in the title, the fewer facts there will be inside.

The third huge economy is on the non-purchase of the device which connects your computer to the phone network – the **modem**, a word which stands not for 'MOdulator-DEModulator' as the books would have you believe, but 'Money Off? Don't Expect Miracles!'

Hooking Up

The next thing you have to avoid is actually getting on-line, which is done via a **service provider**, the service in question usually being to relieve you of a further week's wages and then go bust.

Service providers always give out their e-mail address in preference to their postal address or telephone number. This is so that disgruntled new subscribers, who can't work out how to get a computer connected or haven't yet received the necessary information to do so, can't complain, because they're not yet hooked up to the e-mail system.

Your service provider gives you your e-mail address and can give you your own **domain name** – the bit after the @ – at a price. The one you want will have been taken by someone else, particularly if your name is McDonald or your initials are IBM.

Even with the requisite equipment, the procedure involved in getting your computer hooked up to the Internet is very involved. First, you have to type a very long string of numbers. This is your ID number. Soon after, you have to type another very long string of numbers. This is your telephone bill.

Fortunately, you can use the Internet to arrange a bank loan to cover it. If, that is, you can wait the three hours it takes to get a connection through to the bank's Web site, because all the phone lines are busy with people trying to do the same.

Connection Problems

In fact, up to half of the time, you simply cannot connect with your required destination on the Internet. The server computer you're trying to access may be 'down', which means 'not working'. Or it might be 'busy', which also means 'not working'.

In such a case you have no option but to wait and try later when the phone lines are less jammed. The times to avoid trying to get on the Internet are:

a) Office hours in the UK, where high phone charges and other costs rule out wide domestic use, so most Internet access is done on the sly from computers at work. Around 8 hours per day.

b) Early evenings in Europe, where most access is gained from university computers by students who have finished their day in the lab or the library. The 8 hours following those above.

c) Evenings and early mornings in America, the world's most on-line country, where most Internet access is done from computers at home because of the prevalence of cheap on-line domestic services. The 8 hours preceding those in a).

If anyone you know is having difficulty getting through to any Internet sites, you can confidently tell them to call outside these times, when they will have a much better chance of connection (though it can't be guaranteed).

Telephone Charges

Phone calls through the Internet are effectively only to your service provider's computer, so if that's in your area, all calls – whether to newsgroups in Holland or e-mails to Japan – are at local rates. "That's why the Internet is so popular in America," you can say breezily. "All local calls are free there, you see. Expensive proposition elsewhere, though."

Thus, by remaining unconnected to the Internet, you are in no worse a position than the new Internet user, but have so far saved yourself time and money, to wit:

a) two months' salary
b) two months.

USING THE INTERNET

Once users have the Internet up and running, they will want to know what they can use it for.

Here are nine real-life information areas to give them, with a summary of what the Internet can do in each – which in every case approximates to 'not much'.

News

The immediacy of the Internet makes it ideal for fast information. Weather, for example. Newspapers can only print yesterday's weather. On the Internet, however, you can consult several sites which can actually tell you the weather situation in your area right now. And if you look outside your window, you can see if it is accurate or not.

Other sites can give you 'live' views of the weather in, say, Antarctica or the Gobi Desert. As you can see, such services show off what the Internet does better than any other medium – that is, being impressive, wide-ranging, bang-up-to-the-minute, and futile.

The Internet v Print Media

Newspaper and magazine proprietors are of course very worried about the Internet. Not, as the casual observer might think, because it will supersede the printed medium (television hasn't, and is much cheaper and easier to use than the Internet). The problem for print media, as you can confidently tell people, is that the Internet might put the Internet out of business.

The process is as follows. Newspapers and magazines have to run an Internet site because otherwise they will fall behind their rivals who do. And all those extra staff have to be paid. The trouble is, the proprietors get no money from their Internet edition as it is free, despite its consequent popularity. (On-line newspapers are the most popular and most accessed sites on the Internet.)

So they use it merely as a shop window for the printed, money-earning title, which has to go up in price to finance the Internet edition. So the circulation goes down, and so do profits. Redundancies have to be made, and the first candidates to go are clearly the Internet staff. Thus, the most popular and most accessed Internet sites go out of business.

On-line News Services

The Telegraph, Guardian and *Times* were the first UK papers to go on-line; there are many other news services. The text from the daily editions is not only consultable on the Internet, and cross-referenced so that a story is linked to all related stories, but it is also searchable: you can call up news items about a particular topic or, in the case of *The Guardian*, even search out the items which contain some news.

Internet News's Great Paradox

To access, download and print out the Internet edition takes an hour or two of computer time. Therefore the Internet edition of a newspaper, which is free, costs more than the printed version, which is not.

Music

The Internet is fast-moving without knowing where it's going; bursting full of ideas, all of them other people's; and contains some profound words, never actually combining to form a sentence. All of this makes it ideal for rock and pop music.

Every band, from international million-sellers to back-street hopefuls, has its Web site. You can scan their lyrics, look at their pictures and listen to extracts from their latest album. The more popular the band, the busier their site; the busier their site, the more likely it is that you will not get through or that, if you do get through, there will be a hitch during transmission.

So, if you find the lyrics are meaningless gibberish, the pictures look blurred and hideously coloured, and the music samples are mere noise, then the information is obviously coming across fine.

Playing Sounds

Music or speech can, at a pinch, be relayed 'live' from another computer (a process called 'streaming'). All you have to do is download special add-on programs, though this step will take so long the music will have gone out of fashion by the time you get it.

Otherwise, you have to download the file in silence, store it on your machine, and play it from there. It takes longer to download than it does to play. And takes longer to play than it probably did to write. There is however a bonus: the sound quality is never as good as the original, so much of the detail will be obscured.

Virtually all music samples you hear on the Internet are firmly in copyright, of course, but the record companies tolerate such unauthorised use because it is good publicity. Besides, there would be no point suing: the fans will have spent all their money on maintaining the Web site.

So, you don't need to download all those sound samples; it would take far too long, and the band will no longer be top of the pops by the time you've finished. You just claim you have. "Heard their new album on the Internet," you say in a weary tone. "It's rubbish." In this way you sound well-informed and trendily dismissive. And not only do you save time and money by not going on the Internet; you don't have to buy the album to impress dinner-party guests either.

Musicians

There are thousands of music-related sites on the Internet, some offering sound files for the benefit of musicians in a format called MIDI (musical instrument digital interface) which can be played and edited on synthesisers, in addition to more conventional recorded sound. Several 'virtual bands' exist where a piece of music is downloaded and added to by one musician, then uploaded in its modified form for the next person to add their contribution. As 'artistic differences' – that is, violent arguments – occur in all groups, even with solo artists, the results can be safely waved away.

But one thing is common to all musicians' sites: the extravagant graphics in the home page take even longer to download than the music files.

Internet Music's Great Paradox

If you are a little-known musician, the Internet is an ideal opportunity to display your work. But the more such sites there are, the less the chance of yours being accessed. So the bigger the Internet gets, the smaller your potential audience.

Shopping

The Internet is changing the way we shop. No more rushing home after a frantic dash round the stores and supermarkets. Buying patterns are being revolutionised. More people are now doing things differently. They go for a frantic dash round the stores and supermarkets, and before rushing home, dash round more stores and supermarkets to buy a computer powerful enough to use the Internet.

Internet shopping has been promised for a while now, but we are hardly any nearer to virtual supermarkets, where you explore the aisles in 3D on screen, make selections by clicking on the products you want, see a little shopping-basket graphic pile up with graphics denoting your purchases, and finally fill in your credit card details to pay.

This doesn't stop you claiming to have done so, of course, "in America". (If you do, make up something which went comically wrong: "I selected a crate of Bollinger champagne, fresh strawberries and some Beluga caviar. I had to drive to the post office to collect it, which is just behind the supermarket. When I opened it they'd given me 12 cans of Cherry Coke, a packet of Tortilla chips and a Hershey bar.")

Virtual Money

The big problem is payment. When a supermarket put its wine catalogue on the Internet in 1995, those inspired enough to order a crate had to do so over the telephone. It is perfectly possible to take credit card details over the Internet, but there are disturbing security implications: information can be intercepted en route at any one of the dozens of computers your details might pass through between your home or office and the suppliers of the product.

Scrambling routines are being introduced to circumvent this on so-called 'secure sites', but you can worry anyone who's ever made a credit card transaction over the Internet, secure site or not. Invent stories of people you know who found, a year after ordering a pizza over the Internet, that their credit card statement suddenly included expensive meals in Rio, huge hotel bills in California, and subscriptions to several German-based pornographic journals. And that when they finally sorted it out, a pizza arrived – cold, and with the wrong topping.

If someone mentions e-cash, or on-line currency, or virtual money, or whatever else some pressured journalist invented in last Sunday's paper, insist that such hopes are doomed ("field day for the hackers... easy pickings for loan sharks...money markets and finance thrown into turmoil...computer malfunctions... collapse of Wall Street", etc.).

Buying Goods

Forget everyday shopping. The only buying area the Internet is good for, you can say, is in internationally-based niche markets: "There are reasonable sites for rare classical CDs, out-of-print art books, vintage wines, exclusive holidays, that sort of thing. But hardly mass-market moneyspinners..." This gives you an aura of culture and sophistication without actually costing anything.

If challenged to say where these high-class sites are, say they went out of business because of low sales and credit card fraud. Everyone will believe that.

Internet Shopping's Great Paradox

The more expensive your equipment, the more sophisticated the shopping services you can access. The more opportunities you have to spend your money, the less likely it is that you have any left.

Reference

Standard thinking has it that by the year 2006 we won't have reference books any more: we'll just look everything up on the Internet. This is patent nonsense of course. You know that the reality of the situation is quite the opposite: in fact, the Internet has done wonders for the book industry, spawning thousands of new publications telling people how to use the Internet.

There are unimaginable quantities of information out there on the Internet – quite literally, billions of pages – all of it easily and quickly accessible. It's just that none of it is the information you want.

Finding Information

Suppose, for example, you have need of a simple reference, such as the dates of the Wars of the Roses. All you do is access a Web site called a **search engine** – they are called 'engines' because their main purpose is to conceal your required destinations behind large smokescreens. You run a search for the words 'War' plus 'Roses', and a couple of seconds later, you get a list on the screen detailing thousands of pages on the Internet. You will be just a click away from the Pentagon's plans for World War III, a French horticulturist newsgroup, Wolverhampton War Games Society's Web site, an Australian shower manufacturer's catalogue, every cricket score of Yorkshire v. Lancashire since 1882, the home page of Randall J. Rose Jr. of Newhaven, Connecticut, and so on.

Every conceivable variation on the words you asked for, in fact, apart from the item you require. In the time it took you to start up your computer, connect to the Internet, and access and download the results from the search page, not only could you have looked up the date in a conventional encyclopædia ten times over, but Yorkshire and Lancashire will have completed another cricket match.

Internet Reference's Great Paradox

Between source and public, information gets corrupted by the media. The Internet means it can be accessed directly from source and so be more reliable. But if that single source is tampered with, no-one will have anything to match it against. So the more reliable information sources become, the less trustworthy they are.

Socialising

A new type of socialising has been created by the Internet. You can meet people with some shared interest through newsgroups, perhaps, or from having found their home pages via a search. Then you find they turn into regular correspondents by e-mail, and you have made new friends, spread all around the globe. With one important proviso: you will never meet them. Which is just as well. You wouldn't want to get acquainted with an Internet user who would have you as a friend.

Love on the Internet

An increasing phenomenon of the 1990s has been 'e-mail romance'. More private than a telephone, but more spontaneous than sending memos, e-mail is the ideal way to develop an office relationship into a personal one. It is also much more discreet for having arguments when the affair breaks up. And, if you have been conscientious about filing your e-mails on disc, this forms a valuable body of evidence when the terms of the divorce are to be argued.

E-mail chatups are now so common that it no longer impresses others to say you met your current partner following increasingly steamy on-line exchanges. Put a new twist on it: "Of course, it was e-mail that got us together. We realised we had so much in common when we both voted against implementing it in the office meeting."

Overall, the line to put forward is that you are far too busy to socialise on the Internet because of all your social engagements.

Internet Socialising's Great Paradox

Thanks to the Internet's growing provision for specialist interests, everyone will know more people. But the basis for the relationships will be more and more specific, instead of the broad range of common ground required for deep bonding. So the more acquaintances people make, the fewer friends they will have.

Work

The much vaunted **teleworking** revolution will never come. You can be confident about this, despite what the magazines claim. Those articles saying we'll all soon be working on our computers from our cottages in the country are just wishful thinking by journalists in unpleasantly pokey 40th-floor city offices. Anyone who says teleworking 'is coming' can be stopped by asking them to name a single real person they know who actually does so.

It's a myth, you can say ("proponents fail to address the social aspect of work...team dynamic essential... human interaction evolutionarily necessary for all co-operative activity...anyway teleworking's boring", and so forth).

But the Internet has much to offer the workplace besides e-mail. From the businesses' point of view, economies can be made. The idea is that every Internet connection replaces an administrative job, making the company more efficient. However, each Internet connection also creates at least two technical jobs – for people whose full-time job is to keep the connection working, the Web pages updated, etc. – making the company less efficient.

Video Conferencing

This is sure to get moving soon, probably in a very jerky and unnatural sort of way. On your screen are lots of little windows, each showing live pictures of one of the delegates in their own offices around the world apparently twitching every second or so, and transmitting their speech. In effect, the computer becomes a multi-person videophone, as well as a depressing reminder that whether it's Rome, New York or Tokyo, offices round the world are identical.

The potential for savings is clearly great. Surveys show that around three-quarters of the time taken by business meetings outside the company is wasted in travel there and back. This is eliminated by video conferencing.

The surveys go on to show that the remaining quarter, taken up by the meeting itself, is also wasted, by people just talking to each other. Thus, by forgetting the video conferencing and turning the whole thing over to e-mail, companies can save millions.

Efficiency of Information

Other major efficiencies can be made. Any information which needs regular updating, but also widespread distribution – product catalogues and stock levels, for example – can be stored on one central computer, accessible instantly over the Internet by anyone in the company's various outposts. Material no longer risks being out of date.

It just risks being inaccessible because everyone has to access it from the same computer, so the phone lines are always busy and you can't get a connection.

Internet Work's Great Paradox

Giving workers access to the Internet saves everyone time thanks to e-mail, reference possibilities, centralising of information and so on. People use this spare time to go 'netsurfing', and video conferencing with their friend across the room, costing the company dear in telephone bills and lost productivity. So the more efficient the Internet makes a company, the more wasteful it becomes.

Sex

Far and away the most accessed sites on the Internet are those related to sex. This is a classic illustration of the saying: "Those that can, do. Those that can't, teach. Those that can't teach, write articles about it on the Internet."

There are newsgroups, picture galleries and how-to articles for every orientation, desire, fantasy and fetish possible. And several for those that aren't.

The content of all sites is the same. To get hold of it you have to wait a very long time, and when it does arrive it's disappointing and extremely short. Rather, come to think of it, like…

Sex stories are best avoided, because whatever bizarre and outlandish things you claim to have seen in a newsgroup or pornographic site you have made up, someone else really will have seen something even more bizarre and outlandish. Besides which, you might be thought to fall into the fourth category: "Those that can't even write articles about it on the Internet, browse other people's."

Internet Sex's Great Paradox

Sex-related newsgroups, in stark contrast to all other areas of the Internet, apparently have plenty of uninhibited women willing to engage in intimate e-mail correspondence with eager men. However, on the Internet, it is impossible to tell genders, and pranksters abound. The more forthcoming the 'woman', the more likely it is to be a man.

Advertising

An Internet site costs a company large amounts of money – but however much it is used, they get no money back because there is no practical way of charging for access. So companies are hoping that Internet advertising will enter the scene and finance everything. More and more companies are trendily putting the URLs of their Web sites on their TV and press advertisements.

The problem with this approach is fairly clear, so get in with it quickly. "No-one in their right mind," you say, "is going to start up their computer, access the Internet, type in that URL and wait five minutes for a page of fancy graphics to load, just to get the same ad they've just seen."

Leaving aside the question of whether anyone in their right mind would be on the Internet in the first place, you can proceed to the two options open to advertisers. Either they make their ads interesting, useful, and offer some sort of free gift or other hard benefit, in which case they cost far too much to put together; or they make them appear as part of someone else's well-accessed Web sites, in which case they merely annoy people wanting to use the site.

The second is clearly the way forward on the grounds that if ever advertising is faced with a choice, the more annoying alternative for consumers is the one which is always selected.

Market Research

The Internet is the marketing person's dream. It makes a vast, global, wealthy market instantly accessible, a market which can easily be researched too. When a site is accessed, the computer can tell you which computer has accessed it and when, how long it spent on each page, and which site it visited previously.

If the site forces people to **register**, even more details can be obtained on each person who enters it. The first time you enter a site requiring registration, you are asked to fill in your name, select a password for yourself, and optionally give other details such as your age, job, salary, inside leg, etc.

Having given that, you can enter the site for free merely by giving your password (or by putting a 'bookmark' on the page – that is, telling your computer to keep a note of the URL of this page so you can jump straight to it next time without needing to type anything, and then most probably jump to the next bookmarked page without having read any of it).

Thus, marketing people can provide hitherto unheard-of details to the advertisers. They can then put together stylish, memorable and brilliantly targeted Internet ads which will be totally ignored, because all people want to see on that page is the football results or pictures of their favourite singer, and not a lager advertisement.

If a site requires registration, say it is a mistake: they are putting people off, looking too intrusive and commercial, and losing the goodwill factor the Internet relies on.

If a site does not require registration, say it is a mistake: they are only gaining the casual browser who wouldn't buy anything in any case, looking too amateur, and falling behind what every serious site is doing.

Internet Advertising's Great Paradox

The Internet is a collection of niche markets and, because of the marketing data available, suitable for small-scale, specifically targeted advertisements. But advertising is a big-budget business which depends on mass-market products. The more suitable a product is to be advertised on the Internet, the less likely that it will be.

Home Pages

Visiting someone's **home pages** – their purely personal Web site – is like visiting their front room. It will most probably be untidy, badly maintained, and full of things no-one else would find interesting, such as blurry holiday photographs of them and their friends. This doesn't stop millions of people every year who wouldn't dream of inviting strangers round to their front room from putting their home pages on the Internet.

You can safely ignore home pages; they are scarcely

worth even pretending to have visited. You certainly shouldn't admit to having any. It's possible to rent space to store home pages on a service provider's computer, but they usually go on space 'borrowed' from a university or work server. Those running the server don't generally mind this, because server storage space is vast, and most of the time they can't find enough material to fill it. A bit like the home pages themselves.

Home pages are set up and run enthusiastically for a few months, with a list of favourite REM tracks or other abysmally pointless personal trivia updated every week. Then, when the owner leaves university and loses the free server space, or gets into a relationship and has no time any more, or changes job, or spring arrives, they are abandoned and remain in cyberspace forever, like a time capsule.

Contents

Typically a home page has:

a) too many pictures of the owner

b) a breezy self-description ('Hi! I'm Scott I'm a sophomore at Dementia University North Carolina I like pizzas (<u>click here</u> to see my favourite toppings) and rock music on graduating I hope to be a computer programmer I hope you like my pages <u>click here</u> to e-mail me Scott :-)')

c) long lists of links to a range of quite unrelated Web sites, the only ones which actually work being the most uninspiring ('Here's the home page of my friend <u>Todd</u>, with some neat lists of his favourite REM lyrics...')

d) a few pages related to their hobbies or interests, usually incomplete, with an apologetic 'roadworks' icon ('Available here: <u>Pizzerias of North Carolina</u> complete list, NB this site is still under construction and I only have details on one pizzeria so far but hope it will build up, <u>click here</u> to see my favourite toppings...')

Such hobbies and interests can range from simple hero-worship of pop stars to bizarre illustrated lists of their sexual habits – which could well make you profoundly glad that they *won't* ever invite you into their front room.

Internet Home Pages' Great Paradox

Home pages are the human side of the Internet. One day we will all have them. But everyone's home pages look the same. So the more individual and personal society becomes because of the Internet, the less individual and personal it gets.

SMILEYS

A glance at virtually any e-mail, especially one from America, will show you some odd combinations of colons, dashes and brackets appearing at the end of some paragraphs, the most common being the one here. :-)

These are called **smileys** (or sometimes 'emoticons') because the basic combination – when viewed sideways, like all smileys – resembles the popular 'smiley' badge of the 1970s. Many types of smiley have evolved, most of the more common – and some of the completely contrived – being listed below. Because you can't hear the tone of voice in e-mails (the justification goes) smileys are necessary, to show for example that a remark meant in jest will not be taken the wrong way. In America, whole books listing smileys have been published. "Wonder if :-) counts as a word for the purposes of author payment," you can muse casually.

Denigrate all smileys. They are, you should say, the equivalent of laughing at your own jokes, a poor substitute for being able to convey the right mood using words – as, in fact, writers of 'letters' (an obsolete method of communication now being supplanted by e-mail) used to. ;-)

In fact, to show how the art of correspondence has not just gone to the dogs but has blown its entire pay packet on the last race of the meeting, you can always pretend that you have just received a handwritten letter which featured the infernally grinning symbols.

Besides which, smileys can lead to misinterpretation. Put one at the end of an e-mail saying "Your home pages were every bit as interesting as I expected", for example, and the recipient may be misled into thinking that this was intended as a compliment.

The following list is not for use in your own e-mails, of course; it is merely so you can impress people by saying dismissively "...and he ended his e-mail to me with *this*. Took me half an hour to work out what he meant," and drawing the sequence on the tablecloth or beer mat or whatever. In this way you will appear to have hundreds of eager fans e-mailing you. ?$:- / *

Basic smileys

:-)	Happy
;-)	Winking
:-(	Unhappy
>;->	Devilish wink

More obscure smileys

(-:	Left-handed or Australian
:-o	Shouting
%-(	Spent too long staring at screen
[:-)	Wearing headphones
B-)	Wearing glasses
B:-)	Wearing glasses on top of head
R-)	Glasses broken
:<)	Upper-class
:<)8	Upper-class dressed for dinner
:<)&	Upper-class after a drunken dinner
O-)	Scuba diver
<:-(	Stupid
d:-)	Wearing baseball cap
q:-)	Wearing baseball cap backwards
o:-)	Perfect
:-?	Smoking a pipe

{:-)	Wearing toupee
}:-(	Wearing toupee in an updraft
?$:- / *	Meaningless, but see what you can pass it off as

People

*<:-)	Santa Claus
*:o)	Bozo the Clown
: 8)	Porky Pig
5:-)	Elvis Presley
=):-)	Uncle Sam
=I:-b	Isambard Kingdom Brunel
>>—>.-(	King Harold, 1066
#:o+=	Betty Boop
:-§	Sir Edward Elgar
@%-(	Dmitri Shostakovich
:-©	Al Jolson
: Ω)	Cyrano de Bergerac
:..-(	Paul Gascoigne
)	Cheshire Cat

INTERNET TYPES

Everyone has heard of 'Netsurfers'. But they are only one of five groups of people who use the Internet: Surfers, Paddlers, Divers, Splashers and Sharks. Here is how to spot them.

Surfers

Net activities. They spend their time aimlessly skimming the surface of the Internet, just looking for something interesting. They have many ways of describing it: they surf the Net, they hang out in Cyberspace, they cruise the Infobahn, and similar nonsense. On their home pages they build up huge lists of interesting sites which they have come across, to whose creator they send an e-mail saying something like 'Hey! Just checked out your web site. Cool! Drop in on my home pages at the address below! Greetings from Todd :)', and then never return.

Tell-tale signs. Unbridled enthusiasm about the Internet. Hundreds of indiscriminate links in their home pages to sites which ceased operation three years ago. 'Individual' nom-de-Net such as Cyberpunk, Todd or Nethead.

Internet haunts. Anybody's home pages, once; bizarre sites giving data on how many cans of coke have been sold that day on the campus of El Paso University, once; anything listed in the 'What's Cool' section of the directories; the facility to jump to random pages.

How to stop them e-mailing you. Tell them of this fantastic new site you've found and give a link to something utterly useless like constantly updated live wind speed data from the computer at the summit of Mount McKinley. They will go off in that direction, get distracted by the links to other sites contained in it, and never come back.

Paddlers

Net activities. Paddlers dabble hopefully but never take the plunge. Their home pages are full of enticing-sounding links such as 'Here's a neat list of places to get <u>free tickets to big-name rock concerts</u>' , or 'Here are some <u>video clips of Madonna</u>', but when you click on them you only get a message saying 'Sorry, this site is under construction'. They send you e-mails saying things like 'Love your list of places to visit in the Western Isles of Scotland. Maybe you could add some sound clips, and have an interactive accommodation booking service, and have the tide timetables on-line, updated daily.'

Tell-tale signs. Home pages have little content, only spectacularly ambitious lists of promised facilities. The belief that the Internet will solve all society's problems. Shelves full of 'how to' books and magazines about the Internet which they will get round to reading when they've finished constructing their home pages.

Internet haunts. A different newsgroup every week, where their single contribution sets off a vitriolic argument they never see; anything listed in the 'What's New' section of the directories.

How to stop them e-mailing you. Tell them that you've heard Netscape is beta-testing a top secret **Java** site in America which offers something clearly impossible (three-dimensional colour video, real-time voice-activated translation in 286 languages, etc.). They will go off searching for it and never come back.

Divers

Net activities. Divers have an obsessive desire to get to the bottom of everything; they are the Internet version of computer hackers. They spend hours on other people's web sites, not reading them, but examining how those effects work. Their e-mails quiz you on the equipment, software and techniques you use, and then recommend you some pornographic sites to visit.

Tell-tale signs. Their sites are astonishingly clever. You type in a few details on a ready-made interactive form, click on some locations on a map of the human body, and the site turns them into pornographic animations. Sadly, nobody ever visits them except other Divers, trying to work out how it's done.

Internet haunts. All the Internet pages about the Internet; newsgroups called alt-dot-sex-dot anything.

How to stop them e-mailing you. Tell them there is an amazing interactive hard-core porn video site from Holland which has been censored, but which clever hackers can gain access to by a Perl Script routine hidden in a German-language server in Japan. They will take this as a challenge, go off looking for it and never come back.

Splashers

Net activities. Splashers like causing trouble. Their main activity is sending rude and abusive messages to newsgroups in capital letters, and delighting in the ensuing arguments. They also search the Internet for graphics and text they can steal to put on their own sites.

Tell-tale signs. Home pages full of extremist and inconsistent views, punctuated a) by material which is clearly someone else's copyright – sound samples from their favourite rock albums, pictures taken from magazines etc., and b) badly. Ultra-defensive justification of this when challenged along the lines of 'but the Internet should be free', followed by very threatening copyright notices safeguarding their own material.

Internet haunts. Any newsgroup with a name like alt-dot-political-dot-controversy.

How to stop them e-mailing you. You need two Splashers. (The wait will not be a long one.) E-mail each telling them that the other has called them a schmuck, and stolen material from their site. They will go off in the direction of each other's throats and never come back.

Sharks

Net activities. Sharks see every Internet site as an opportunity to advertise their small businesses. They invariably supply tosh, such as cassettes with 'subliminal messages' to 'stop you smoking' or 'empower you as a creative individual'. They spend their on-line lives sending e-mails and posting messages to newsgroups which start 'Hi! I'm Scott from California. Love your web home page!' and end 'Send your credit card details NOW and within seven days you will receive our exclusive Creative Empowerment Cassette™ as the first step in the Personal Enrichment Program®™©...'

Tell-tale signs. Worryingly high frequency in their messages of words such as 'subliminal', 'credit card details', and 'hello'.

Internet haunts. Any newsgroup they think might have a good proportion of gullible, immature users with more money than sense – that is, any newsgroup.

How to stop them e-mailing you. Tell them of this wonderful newsgroup you've heard of whose title you're not exactly sure of, but it's something like alt dot gullible dot rich. They will go off in desperate search of it and never come back.

THE FUTURE

What will become of the Internet? No-one has the first idea, so you can say what you like.

Things develop on the Internet at an incredible pace. A development in normal computing – a new version of a popular word processor or picture manipulation program, for example – might take a year or two, perhaps several, to establish itself generally. On the Internet, because almost any new program or technological widget can be downloaded in a free working version straight away, the time-lag between availability of finished product (or more usually, half-finished product, the so-called 'beta test' version) and its establishment in the mainstream can be as little as a month or two.

So if you're talking to someone and they start enthusing about some specific technical development ('Hey! I've heard that Sun's HotJava browser on Windows NT 3.5 can run Java applets enabling me to put in animations!') then reply that:

a) it's already old-fashioned and outdated ("Yes, well, of course, Java's been around for a while now, and it's showing its age... everyone's hoping its short-comings will be put right by the update when that comes out.")

b) it has been widely misused, to the detriment of the Internet ("Now every Web site has a half-hour greeting sequence of a grinning programmer's face drivelling on at you, with animation like a strobe light. It's infuriating.")

But generally people do not want to talk specifics. They want the grand picture. Dinner party talk is rarely about the exciting possibilities offered by dynamic HTML, or database versus static pages. It is about whether the Internet Is Any Good, and Where It Is Going, and other such sentiments with too many capital letters.

So you can choose any of the following, depending on the company you wish to impress, the weather, your mood or England's last performance at Wembley. Remember the capital letters:

a) The World will be a Better Place. By 2006, everyone in the world will be on-line. The Internet will make shops, offices and all non-leisure travel unnecessary, and because of the savings, everything will be free. Wars will end. Everyone will be happy.

b) The World will be a Worse Place. By 2006, everyone in the West will be on-line, but the growing billions of third world poor will still live in poverty. The resulting instability will cause worldwide war, and the third world scientists will learn how to make nuclear bombs through the Internet. Everyone will die.

c) Governments will Take Over the Internet. By 2006, Big Brother really will be able to watch you. All your e-mails, bank details, personal schedules – everything will be recorded and scrutinised. Internet computers will all be fitted with cameras to monitor the owner 24 hours a day. Totalitarian regimes will come into power everywhere. Everyone will be oppressed.

d) The People will Take Over the Internet. By 2006, the sheer volume of Internet traffic will mean government control of individuals will be impossible. Effectively self-governing little societies will spring up with people living in 'virtual villages'. Everyone will be free.

e) The Internet is a passing fad. By 2006, the novelty value will have worn off. It will be thought of much like the fax machine: useful in its own way, but hardly life-changing. Everyone will go about their business just as before.

The most likely outcome is of course e), in which case you will have saved approximately a years' salary by buying this book and not having joined the Internet in the first place.

The Internet is one of life's certainties. It is coming to all of us. And as it gets bigger, its name gets shorter.

In 1969, the 'Defense Advance Research Projects Agency Net' consisted of four US military computers, the technological equivalent of tin cans joined by a string.

At the beginning of the 1990s, a handful of private computer users joined the few thousand-strong network of business, academic and military machines, and the name 'Computer Internet' was steadily trimmed to 'the Internet'.

In mid-1997, some 50 to 80 million regularly used the system increasingly just called 'the Net', or even, shrinking its capital letter, 'the net'.

By the year 2006, everyone in the world will be connected to everyone else at least twice, and its name will consist solely of trendy white space. You will socialise and have sex over your computer screen, go on holiday without leaving your desk, and have arguments with thousands of people you've never met. All on an entity which doesn't even have a name any more, so can't be to blame for anything.

GLOSSARY

Applet – Programming nugget written in Java, often involving graphics, animation and visuals (as in 'some appletart, please').

ASCII – American Standard Code for Information Interchange, pronounced 'ass-key': the set of characters in e-mails (just A-Z, a-z, 0-9, and a few punctuation marks) which force any European language in the world to be reproducible on the typewriter keyboard, and thus incomprehensible.

Baud rate – Speed at which Internet information is passed through the phone lines to your computer, and hence how fast you find it becomes tedious: 14400 is just dreary; 28800 completely stultifying.

Bulletin board – E-mail on-line conference between computer users discussing topics usually low on general interest which lays itself open to yet another desperate pun on 'bored'.

Cybercafé – Café with Internet computers you can hire by the hour and use to order pizzas.

Dot – Part of a URL or e-mail address. Say 'dot' not 'full stop' or 'period'. And that's all there is to it. Period.

FAQ – Frequently Asked Questions; the part of a site where useful answers to typical newcomers' questions appear – e.g. 'How can I find this FAQ page?'.

Flaming – Sending abusive messages over the

Internet. Half of all flames are replies to other flames, usually using bad language to complain about the bad language used. The other half are sent to incite such replies.

HTML – Hyper Text Mark-up Language: verbose layout instructions inside < > marks, used to create Web pages and link them to others. Also stands for Horribly Tangled Messy Language.

Hypertext – Hyperactively underlined words in Web pages which, when clicked on, take you to other Web pages.

Internet Explorer – Microsoft's Web browsing software. Always called 'IE', like the Latin abbreviation, because users feel they have to keep explaining themselves.

IP – Internet Protocol, one of many techie abbreviations you can pepper your conversation with at random to confuse people without having to know what it means. Similarly TCP (Transmission Control Protocol) SLIP (Serial Line Internet Protocol) and PPP (Point to Point Protocol).

IRC – Internet Relay Chat, which lets you have real-time typed 'conversations' over the Internet with like-minded people – for example, someone sitting opposite you in the cybercafé.

ISDN – Integrated Services Digital Network, a super-fast digital phone line which dispenses with the need for modems and therefore costs several times as much.

Java – A language enabling browsers to do wonderful things, like display animations of coffee being poured out.

Microsoft network – The Internet service provided to Windows 95 owners and built in to new PCs as part of Bill Gates's 'road ahead'. If you have Gates on a road ahead, as any walker could tell you, there will be no style.

Netiquette – Guidelines on correct net behaviour, most stunningly obvious, such as 'try to write comprehensible English if possible' and 'don't abuse or libel other Internet users unless they attack you first'.

Netscape – Company which makes Navigator, the rival to Internet Explorer. Downloadable free (for trial) over the Internet but, by the time it arrives, that version is out of date.

Neuromancer – Title of a book written in 1984 by American author William Gibson which popularised the terms 'cyberspace', 'jacking into the Net', etc.

Newbie – Any beginner on the Internet sufficiently new to think that a decent, sensible, polite question posted to a newsgroup will get a decent, sensible, polite answer.

POP – Point of [Internet] Presence, the location of the nearest server to you – not 'point' as in 'what is the'.

Server – Computer which serves up information to

the Internet, faster than Boris Becker, but also quicker to fall down.

SIG – Special interest group, the topic always being something uninteresting like computers.

Spamming – Sending the same irritating message to newsgroups repeatedly and indiscriminately (from the obsessive repetition of the word 'spam' in a Monty Python sketch).

Transmission interrupted – Common error message when the Internet page you are trying to access comes across incompl

UNIX – System used by servers; often pronounced 'eunuchs' because of the uncertainty of having any successors.

VRML – Virtual Reality Modelling Language, used to create artificial Internet worlds depicting any sort of fantasy situation – for example, one in which newsgroups are polite and helpful to newcomers.

Webmaster – Those who look after a site, though all they spin are tales to explain why it hasn't been updated for three months.

WWW – Short form for World Wide Web, and typical of many computing terms in that its 'abbreviation' is less comprehensible and actually takes longer to say.

THE AUTHOR

Rob Ainsley was created at 4.40 p.m. on 3 Sep 1960 in Hull and last updated sometime in 1987. He is always inaccessible because he is 'busy', though busy doing what is not clear – like most of the world's Internet servers, in fact.

Editor for many years of the monthly magazine *Classic CD*, he runs ClassicalNet UK, a Web site on classical music with up-to-the-minute news items ('Beethoven still dead', etc.) and a site for visitors to his adopted home town ('Budget Guide – Bath on $800 a day' and so on).

Despite stiff competition from Internet experts worldwide, he was selected to write this book because he was one of the few candidates not to believe everything that has been written about the Internet.

If you would like to write to him, perhaps with observations on discrepancies in the spec of HTML 3.0 or comments on the cross-platform implementation of Java applets, send your e-mail to rob@bluffers.co.uk. It won't get anywhere, because that isn't a real address, but you will feel better for getting it off your chest.

– Ends –

THE BLUFFER'S GUIDES™

Available at £1.99*, £2.50 and £2.99:

Accountancy
Advertising
Archaeology
Astrology & Fortune Telling*
Ballet*
Bluffing
Champagne
Chess
The Classics
Computers
Consultancy
Cricket
Doctoring
Economics
The European Union
Finance
The Flight Deck
Golf
The Internet
Jazz
Law
Music
Management

The Occult*
Opera
Paris
Philosophy
Photography*
Marketing
Public Speaking
Publishing*
The Quantum Universe
The Races
The Rock Business
Rugby
Science
Secretaries
Seduction
Sex
Skiing
Small Business
Tax
Teaching
University
Whisky
Wine

All these books are available at your local bookshop or newsagent, or by post or telephone from: B.B.C.S., P.O.Box 941, Hull HU1 3VQ. (24 hour Telephone Credit Card Line: 01482 224626)

Please add the following for postage charges: UK (& BFPO) Orders: £1.00 for the first book & 50p for each additional book up to a maximum of £2.50; Overseas (& Eire) Orders: £2.00 for the first book, £1.00 for the second & 50p for each additional book.